Best
Funeral
Meditations

CSS Publishing Company, Inc., Lima, Ohio

BEST FUNERAL MEDITATIONS

Scripture quotations marked (NRSV) are from the *New Revised Standard Version of the Bible*, copyright 1989 by the Division of Christian Education of the National Council of the Churches of Christ in the USA. Used by permission.

Scripture quotations marked (RSV) are from the *Revised Standard Version of the Bible*, copyrighted 1946, 1952 © 1971, 1973, by the Division of Christian Education of the National Council of the Churches of Christ in the USA. Used by permission.

Scripture quotations marked (NIV) are taken from the *Holy Bible, New International Version*. Copyrighted © 1973, 1978, 1984 International Bible Society. Used by permission of Zondervan Bible Publishers. All rights reserved.

Scripture quotations marked (TLB) are taken from *The Living Bible* © 1971. Used by permission of Tyndale House Publishers, Inc., Wheaton, IL 60189. All rights reserved.

Scripture quotations marked (KJV) are from the *King James Version of the Bible*, in the public domain.

Library of Congress Cataloging-in-Publication Data

Best funeral meditations : an anthology.
    p.   cm.
  ISBN 0-7880-1159-6 (pbk.)
  1. Funeral sermons. 2. Sermons, American.
BV4275.B47   1998
252'.1—dc21   97-18443
                                                              CIP

This book is available in the following formats, listed by ISBN:
    0-7880-1159-6   Book
    0-7880-1160-X IBM 3 1/2
    0-7880-1161-8   MAC
    0-7880-1162-6   Sermon Prep

PRINTED IN U.S.A.

Shout for joy, O heavens;
rejoice, O earth;
burst into song, O mountains!
For the Lord comforts his people
and will have compassion
on his afflicted ones.

Isaiah 49:13 (NIV)

Table of Contents

Preface

Best Funeral Meditations is an anthology of sermons for a variety of situations. The anthology begins with a sermon on the subject of death preached by a noted minister on a college campus during Holy Week. It concludes with a sermon, written by one of CSS Publishing's best-known authors, which could be preached at any funeral. In between are eighteen meditations preached on the deaths of young children, of elderly, lifelong church members, of a non-Christian, of a person the minister did not know, and of accident victims. Two of the sermons include the order of worship, and two others suggest appropriate hymns which might be used during the service.

We believe that this collection will help the pastor meet the challenges of simultaneously preparing for ministry to those who are bereaved and proclaiming the Good News to those who are engulfed in sorrow.

Meditations in this anthology were selected from recent submissions to CSS Publishing and from past collections of funeral sermons.

1

When We
See Death

Harold C. Warlick, Jr.

2 Corinthians 4:7-12

Some years ago, I was asked to preach for a week-long series of services in First Baptist Church, Fort Myers, Florida. I pulled together a dozen of what I considered to be my *best* sermons, threw them in a briefcase, and our family boarded a jet to Florida. The morning of the first service I stood by the organ with the guest musician, my friend William Brown, as he shuffled through his musical selections, trying to mesh their themes with my sermons. Now, unbeknown to me at that time, over 75 percent of the population in that section of Florida is over seventy years of age. The front doors to the sanctuary flung open and the people started piling in. By the time worship started there were over 500 people in the sanctuary, and it appeared to me that fewer than five percent were under seventy years old.

As the organist began the prelude, William Brown walked across the platform to my chair and whispered into my ear, "Man, we are in trouble. We are in trouble!" And he was right. All my sermons were either generalized appeals to "love thy neighbor and recommit your life to a more purposeful future" or a harsh call to involvement in building a better world. His musical selections were in the same vein. But if life is a journey or a pilgrimage, as the preachers and teachers tell us, then that audience was at a point of hearing a word from the conductor calling to collect their tickets.

9

So Brown sang "Nobody Knows The Trouble I've Seen, Nobody Knows But Jesus," and I preached from memory, as best I could, a sermon on the resurrection.

We preachers do not preach on death very often, especially on a college campus. Most of my own sermons are appeals to find scriptural resources for dealing with the harsh realities of daily living, for finding grace sufficient to forgive personal sins, or for generalized appeals to "get with it, you nineteen-year-olds."

Sometimes life causes us to have to change focus and look at death even before a good bit of the sand has dropped in our personal hourglass of life. There is nowhere on any campus to hide from the reality of death. Will Kime, a guest speaker in our auditorium, once asked all students who had experienced the death of a brother or sister or a friend their age to raise their hands. Over half of our students put them up. And in the last two months we have memorialized two students, one in the day and one in the EDP, who died tragically at much too young an age.

This is the time of year, the week before Holy Week, that the Church turns its seasonal calendar to focus on death. The Cross of Christ represents the reality of the ugliness and despair in life. It is a reality from which no one can escape. Much too soon, we will *all* see death.

Perhaps it is a proper time for us to see death, for most of us have some years left to transform our life's meaning. Alfred Bernhard Nobel became an inventor and chemist in the mid-1800s. In 1863 he patented a mixture of nitroglycerin and gunpowder. Three years later his big invention came when he invented dynamite. His renown as the inventor of dynamite became worldwide. Later in his life he received quite a shock. While reading the morning newspaper he saw on the front page the headline "Alfred Nobel Dead." The sub-headline read "Dynamite King Dies." The article referred to him as "the merchant of death" and "Inventor of Destruction."

Nobel was obviously appalled as he read a description of the impression he had left the world by his invention. As it turned out, an overly eager reporter in France had seized upon news of the death of another Alfred Nobel, of no relation, and flashed it across the telegraph wires, trying to beat his fellow reporters to the punch.

The real Alfred Nobel was completely shaken and unnerved as he stared into death. He realized for the first time that he would be remembered only as a man who spread death and destruction everywhere. Surely, he thought, this was not the aim of a worthy life. He knew he had to transform his purpose and make a contribution to the life of the world. Consequently he dedicated his great fortune to peace among the nations and founded the annual Nobel Peace Prize. Now Alfred Nobel's name is associated with the winners of this prize, like the Red Cross, Martin Luther King, Jr., and Albert Schweitzer.

Death can wake us up to a transformation of our life's meaning. Its awareness can turn useless lives into those which are very, very useful. The ashes on the forehead on Ash Wednesday, the cross on the altar, and the memorial service next Wednesday when the names of friends of ours who died since last Easter will be in the bulletin, all have their role to play in our awareness. As much as we would like to run from it, we must all see death.

One day in college, my roommate came back to the residence hall completely shaken. He was president-elect of the student body and the university had brought in a consultant to talk with the new Student Government Association officers about leadership. This consultant did not give a speech. He didn't say a word. He just loaded them in a car and drove them a few miles into the woods. There beside the road was a freshly dug grave. He made them all get out of the school van and stand around the empty hole. He said, "I want you to look into that hole, keep it in mind, and think of it as you make plans for the new year. Look backwards from this hole and enjoy life, rejoice in your fellow students, and remember to really live because one day you'll be in a hole just like this one."

They got back in the van and drove back to campus; and no one said a word. He let them out in front of their residence halls, one-by-one. End of retreat, good-bye consultant. It has been almost thirty years and I can still remember how profound an impact that experience had on my roommate. When you envision the rest of your life and work backward to the present it has a profound transformation on your life. This has a keen influence on college students who think death is something that happens to others and is always a million years away.

If the life of the human race from its creation to the present could be captured on motion picture films, all the frames in that film combined would not add up in importance to the one where this Jesus of Nazareth cried, "It is finished," and pitched his head forward in death on the cross. That crucifixion took nearly nine hours. It was a slow death, the muscles degenerating into knobs of agony. There was nothing civilized about it. Paul tells us, "God was in Christ reconciling the world ..." (2 Corinthians 5:19). Think of it. God — hanging like a slab of meat on some spikes. Most of the faithful never showed up. Those who came were for the most part ignorant hecklers who spat and cursed. God in Christ looked down on a scene of madness, cried, "It is finished," and slumped over into eternity. That is a vision that you and I should keep before ourselves. The cross of death has the power to transform life in the present. When one realizes that death has been conquered, the freshly dug grave of our own demise can have the power to make an improvement in the way we manage life today. We have to see death, reflect upon it, and hold ourselves beside it to see the way it can change us. We have to see death in order to know that Christ has overcome it. We have to see ourselves as ultimately cast down but not destroyed in order to reveal to ourselves who we really are.

There was a great fire in Boston in the 1920s that helped to prolong your life and my life. Because of that destruction, that death, you and I live longer lives. The fire swept away a whole block of valuable property. Newspaper man Russell Conwell went over to the ruins for the purpose of making a report to his paper concerning it.[1] He had been up the whole night because the fire was a tremendous one and had destroyed millions of dollars worth of property. As he stood at the corner of Franklin and Pearl streets, everything was in ruins. There was nothing but ashes for a whole block. The owner had put a sign on a rough board and stuck it up in the middle of the ashes. It was a quotation from 2 Corinthians: "Cast down but not destroyed." As the owner of the block stood there with the reporter, he had lost everything except the cellar of a store in the corner next to Pearl Street. As the citizens began to rummage curiously through the debris, a man, in great excitement, ran up to the policemen on the scene. Some drugs had been stored in the cellar. And the fire had produced many great changes among them. In fact, the changes were so great this professor ordered the police to guard the cellar while chemists from a nearby university could get over there and examine the great results that had been accomplished by the awful and continuous heat of so many hours' duration. Out of that examination came a far greater wealth than the owner had ever imagined.

Out of the known combinations which heat will make of chemicals and minerals so deposited as they were at the time of this fire, there came an almost complete scientific revolution. Two months after the fire, *Popular Science Monthly* and *Scientific Weekly* published a long list of improvements, which that fire revealed, in the management and discoveries of chemistry.[2] You and I go to bed tonight with the hope of a longer life because drugs are available to us that emerged from being held for so long and so close to destruction. Our whole physical prospect for life was transformed into something greater.

Take this Easter and hold yourself close to the cross. Don't turn away from the harshness of death. Let it shake you, and look deep into your own heart. If you wear a cross around your neck, play with it. Twirl it in your fingers and see death. Stand close to the reality of death and see it. Look at the cross sitting on the altar and on the pulpit. Look at these stained-glass windows and see death. Only when you see death can you appreciate the victory we have in Christ. Start with the end of your life and work back to today. What is the aim of a worthy life? What improvements and discoveries are to be made by you? Stand close to the destruction and let it pass over you. Your whole outlook will be transformed into something more useful. You cannot have life in you unless you have death in you. The resurrection cannot be real to you unless the cross is real to you. "We always carry around in our body the death of Jesus, so that the life of Jesus may also be revealed in our body" (2 Corinthians 4:10, NIV).

When we seek death we can smile and see that "it is finished!" So be it!

---

1. Russell H. Conwell, *Borrowed Axes* (Philadelphia: Judson Press, 1923), pp. 78-79.

2. *Ibid.*

Dr. Harold C. Warlick, Jr., is Chair of the Department of Religion and Minister to the University at High Point University, High Point, North Carolina.

2

Loaned
Or Owned?

Ole Winter

---

2 Samuel 12:18-23 (RSV)

The story is told of a king who came visiting another monarch as a gesture of friendship, and all was done according to the protocol of that nation. As the visiting king was leaving he was given, as a parting gift, a beautiful and exotic tropical plant. It came in a very large planter, and the entire entourage could see that it was ready to bloom.

When the king arrived at his own palace he instructed his head gardener to tend the plant so that it could show off its lovely flower. He had been told that the bud, which would burst into bloom, was the most beautiful flower in the world. The gardener did as he was told; in fact, he took care of it better than any other plant in the king's expansive garden. He watered and fertilized it with the appropriate minerals, and the bud grew larger and larger. One day the gardener went out of his way to tell the king that it might bloom by the next morning.

But early the next morning, when the gardener ran to see how the blossom looked, the pot with the flower was missing from its special place. The gardener was beside himself! What in the world could he tell the king? He had done all that he was instructed to do; but he knew that his monarch was a stern man who was not beyond punishing him for such an irresponsible act as losing a potted plant.

15

But he had no choice, and he quickly went to report the loss to the king in his chambers.

As he was admitted into the king's presence, there stood the plant with the monarch. Together with all of his family and advisors they stood admiring the fantastic bloom which had exploded from the plant overnight. The gardener was of course relieved, but at the same time he was a bit disappointed. He had so much wanted to be the first to tell the king. But then he realized that the plant had only been loaned to him for a short while to be cared for. It really was the king's very special plant, and when it blossomed and burst forth into its full destiny as a flower, the king wanted it in his own chambers.

_____ and _____, this story of the king and his lovely flower is also the way it is with our children. They are given to us as a "loan" for a while. We, like the gardener, have them entrusted into our care for a short time. Then they blossom and they are gone! _____ was surely your child! But because of his death at such a very young age you didn't even have time to get acquainted with him. Surely he was your child; he was born of your union and your oneness in love. But in another sense he was never yours. He was given to you as a loan for a short while. In this case he left you much sooner than most children leave their parents, for he left you in death. But when _____ was baptized, he was adopted into the family of God! You were entrusted to care for him and watch over him as he needed it. But very much like that plant, he came to an early bloom. And he is now in the presence of the king!

It is so difficult for us to know why some make it into and through this world in the biblical "three score years and ten," while others are something like the insect that hatches and dies literally within hours. This is one of those things for which we have no answer, and in this life never really will.

But in this case the story of the king and his special flower may help us. For though _____ was really not more than a tiny bud on the stem of life, we have the promise that he is now in full bloom in the King's presence.

Our God is a gracious God! But his ways are not our ways and our ways are not his! Thank him for that, because if things always went our way, this would be a very, very sorry world. So God has ways and plans that we know nothing about. God does have ways and plans that we know plenty about and we learn from them. But other times we seem unable to solve the puzzles of this life.

I suppose we could say, "But _____ just barely had time to be alive!" Yes, but in another sense he never died. When I came to the hospital and there was concern for this tiny one, we decided it would be prudent to have a baptism then and there! In that sterile environment, with the assistance of a Roman Catholic Sister, _____ was adopted into the King's family. The bud of his new life in Christ began to grow. And now we know that he is in the palace of the King.

Maybe you recall that there was a king in the Old Testament who lost a "flower" which was about to bloom. That, of course, was King David of Israel. The child which Bathsheba bore in their relationship was so seriously ill shortly after birth that on the seventh day of his short life he died. King David was so distraught and anxious that his servants and counsellors were afraid of what he might to do himself when they told him the baby had died. For days, as the baby lay struggling for life, he had prayed that God might spare the child; but it did not happen. Finally one of his trusted advisors told David, "The child is dead!"

Then David did a strangely wonderful thing. Hear what the Bible says about it: "Then David arose from the earth, and washed, and anointed himself, and changed his clothes; and he went into the house of the Lord, and he worshiped; then he went to his own house; and when he asked, they set food before him, and he ate." In other words, David moved out of the "sackcloth and ashes" mode and cleaned himself up. We would say he got up, took a shower, shaved, and put on clean clothes. To say the least the king's servants were a bit puzzled; in fact, they were confused and said as much. "What is this thing that you have done? You fasted and wept for the child while it was alive; but when the child died you arose and ate food." They thought he had nearly gone mad during the child's illness and now he was acting completely normal. David

17

answered them this way, "While the child was still alive, I fasted and wept; for I said, 'Who knows whether the Lord will be gracious to me, that the child may live?' But now he is dead; why should I fast? Can I bring him back again? I shall go to him, but he will not return to me." King David, it seems, was at least two things. He was a believer and he was a realist. What he did surely was questioned by other faithful believers! But he understood that that child had now been put into the palace of an eternal king; he could no longer be in this earthly kingdom of his.

In your case, _____ was with you even less than the seven days of King David's newborn! _____ was not able to bring you those smiles, that laughter, and, yes, also the tears that a surviving child would have. We know that every child brings to us both the smiles and the tears.

But now, as did King David, it is time to commit _____ into the hands of our loving God and Father! It is time to think of him like the plant that has blossomed overnight and is now in the King's palace. It is time to begin to let him go.

I know that you realize it, but hear it again! _____ became a part of the family of God even though he did not know it in a cognitive way! He was made a child of God in baptism, but he knew nothing of it. And yet he was as much a child of God as are you and I who can name the day of our baptism.

So as the gardener had to let that beloved and much cared for plant go into the king's palace, so we must do with _____. We need to let him go to and with God. There need be no guilt on your part! Oh, there may be those times that you will think, "Oh ... but wasn't there something we could have done!" There needs be no blame. The kind of world in which we live sees these kinds of things happen. Comparatively some of us live as long as the redwood trees and others are like the mayfly that spends an hour or two before death.

Now we can do nothing more than did David. We can and will rely on the promises of God and the hope he gives us. So like David, as soon as we can, it is time to get ourselves "cleaned up." It is appropriate to go into the house of the Lord as did David. We do that even now in this memorial service. Then David gathered his wits about him and went on with his life.

Oh, yes, I think it is important to remember that the Bible also says this: "Then David comforted his wife Bathsheba...." Now they did not benefit from all the psychological training we have. They did not have magazines and books to tell them how to get through a time of grief. But in that society where the king hardly ever talked to his queen, it seems that David went out of his way to help her through this time of loss as well. He did the right and loving thing. _____ and _____, this is the time for you to spend much time with each other to talk about this terrible loss. It is time to comfort one another.

By the way, none of what is said in 2 Samuel seems to indicate that David did not care! Far from it! In fact, this biblical passage seems to bend over backward to show how much he really did care. But this shepherd turned king had not forgotten that God was with him not only as the shepherd boy, but as the king who had suffered a great loss. And so he spoke of hope. "I shall go to him, but he will not return to me." As much as he would like it, the baby would not come back to him! But even as limited as was the Old Testament hope of life after death, David was convinced he would go to be with his child one day.

Now we have the same hope! And we have it even so much more clearly than did David, for we look at life through the windows of Good Friday and Easter. We have the hope of a God who loved us even to death itself! We have the hope of Christ who walked out of that tomb with the promise that we will truly walk one day with one another in a new life.

It is now up to us to trust God as did King David. It is up to us to show that hope, that trust, and that love to those around us who are hurting so much. Yes, life will one day return to normal! Oh, I am sure that you will never quite be the same! No one ever really is who loses an infant! It will be important for you as parents to care for your other children, and let them know that you love them as much as the one who died.

_____ was never really yours! For just a few fleeting hours he was with you, just long enough to receive your name! But

19

more important than you giving him a name is the promise that God has given him his name and ushered him into his presence. The King has a place for him. And now in "full bloom," he stands in the Father's house. Comfort one another with these thoughts. Amen.

After 37 years as a pastor of the Evangelical Lutheran Church in America in California and Iowa, Ole Winter is retired. He works part-time as an Advocate for Lutheran Social Service of Iowa.

3

Death Shows
No Partiality

James W. Robinson

Death is no respecter of persons. Death shows no partiality. That is something I have learned over the years. I have looked down at the sweet doll-like faces of infants moments after death has snatched them from their mothers' arms. I have seen the sleep of death steal over the five-year-old victim of an arsonist. I have cried in the night over a 25-year-old friend crushed to death by a tractor. My wife and I wept for hours the night we were informed that our nineteen-year-old son had been cut down by a bullet in a war-torn country far from home. I have shared the last moments of men and women in their forties and fifties. I have watched good and kind people go down to their graves before their time. Death is no respecter of persons. It matters not what their age or station in life may be. Hardest of all to endure is the death of a little child. What a cruel blow that the curtain should come down prematurely with the words, "The End," emblazoned upon it!

"The End." Do you believe that? I do not! Death does not have the final say. Death may write the words, "The End," on the curtain, but God walks through that curtain as if it were not even there. He comes to escort his children beyond the curtain, to a stage set with the furniture of home.

Eternal life adds sense to existence. Somewhere, beyond the curtain, God has prepared a place where people are made whole and are healed, and their lives are made complete. The child who

21

died in the crib, the youth killed in an automobile accident, the soldier cut down by a bullet go on to grow in the presence of God. The mentally retarded and the physically handicapped go on to receive clear minds and healthy bodies. The sick and the distressed who die before their time go on to be restored to the life with God that is life indeed. They live in the freedom of a spiritual existence. Their bodies are changed; they drop the robe of flesh; they are given spiritual bodies adapted for a spiritual existence. The Bible tells us that in that place — the place we call heaven — God "will wipe away every tear from their eyes, and death shall be no more, neither shall there be mourning nor crying nor pain any more, for the former things have passed away."

I know that my words may sound empty and hollow, but your little boy is in the best of hands. He is going to have the time of his life. He's going to be with his heavenly Father. He is going to be in the presence of perfect love. He is going to be with Jesus, who loved little children more than anyone else in the world. He is going to have more friends than he ever had in this life. And he is going to grow, and God is going to give him things to do that will make him happy for eternity.

Tommy's parents and brothers and sisters are going to miss him greatly. I say this because I know how it feels to miss a child, even though I had mine with me for a few more years than you had yours. You must be prepared to weep again and again. At times you will weep when you least expect sadness to steal over you, when you are not even thinking of your absent little boy.

But there will be occasions when you will smile as you fondly remember certain little things about him. And you will thank God that you had him, if only for a little while. Someday, the heavy burden of grief will lighten, and you will be able to carry it more easily. And God will use this dark experience to help you lighten the load of others who walk through the valley of the shadow of death.

When my wife and I lay on our beds that first night, mourning the death of our son, we received a telephone call at midnight. A chaplain friend was on the line. He had served with the Marines during wartime. Twice he had nearly lost his legs from exploding mines. "Jim," he said, "I want to help. I'll come to you, if you'd like me to. I'll get on the plane, right now, and I'll stay with you as long as you need me."

That is what God is saying to you at this very moment. I realize it is difficult for you to hear his voice. But he's saying, "I'm coming to you. I'm with you now. I'm here to help. I'm here to stay." You must believe that, and accept his offer, or *you will not make it.* With his help, you will find that you can make it and will make it and be better parents to your remaining children than you were before this happened.

John Greenleaf Whittier wrote this poem. It has comforted many since it was first written. I hope that it will comfort you, and that it will help you take a bolder look at the future.

I know not what the future hath
of marvel or surprise,
Assured alone that life and death
His mercy underlies.

And if my heart and flesh are weak
to bear an untried pain,
The bruised reed he will not break
But strengthen and sustain.

And so beside the Silent Sea
I wait the muffled oar;
No harm from him can come to me
On ocean or on shore.

I know not where his islands lift
Their fronded palms in air;
I only know I cannot drift
Beyond his love and care.

This poem is not only for your little boy. He is more alive than we. It is for you, the living in this world. You will never drift, you "cannot drift beyond his love and care."

You will see your little boy again in the happiest of your memories, and later on as you play with him on the sand "where his islands lift their fronded palms in air."

(Reprinted from "The Beauty Of Being Prepared," by James W. Robinson, CSS Publishing Company, Inc., © 1982.)

4

No Easy Words
Of Comfort

David A. MacLennan

Matthew 18:10 (RSV)

Jesus said, "See that you do not despise one of these little ones; for I tell you that in heaven their angels always behold the face of my Father who is in heaven."

When a little child dies, no easy words comfort us. Even to the strong Christian believer, the death of a child seems so senseless, so wasteful, so inconsistent with all we know of our heavenly Father. Jesus loved and welcomed little children. He made them the type of person who is fit for the Kingdom of Heaven. "Truly, I say to you, unless you turn and become like children, you will never enter the kingdom of heaven," he said (Matthew 18:3). Yet today we are met to worship God who is love and to pay our tribute of love to a child suddenly taken from the family where she was so much loved. Before life's day had scarcely begun for Martha, it seems to have ended cruelly. What can we say to lessen the grief of hearts sorely hurt by this sorrow? Rather, what can the Lord himself say to them and to us to lighten the burden of bereavement, and to brighten the darkness of our souls?

First, Jesus our Lord speaks the same words of assurance he spoke during his earthly life. "And calling to him a little child, he put him in the midst of them, and said, 'Truly, I say to you, unless you turn and become like little children, you will never enter the kingdom of heaven. Whoever humbles himself like this child, he is the greatest in the kingdom of heaven!' " To be like children is to have many lovely characteristics — the capacity to wonder, to forgive easily, to forgive the pain and heartache, to love freely those who are loving, to play. You may be sure that this dear girl is at home in what a poet called "the nurseries of heaven."

To be as a child is to be dependent. Just as she depended on her parents so, in the unseen home God prepares for all who love him, she will depend on the love and care of the One who loves little children and loves them forever.

Again, we should be comforted by Christ's beautiful affirmation: "for I tell you that in heaven their angels always behold the face of my Father who is in heaven." The New English Bible translators give the translation "their guardian angels" (Matthew 18:10). Jesus had issued a stern warning to anyone who "causes one of these little ones who believe in me to sin." He also spoke encouragingly to those who welcome a child and who love him or her and help the child to know God. This, said our Savior, is to welcome and help Christ himself. The best teacher and helper of a child is the Christian mother in the home, or the one who has taken the mother's place. Even though Martha has left her mother for a time, the mother's reward is great.

More so than most people today, the ancients believed that every child had its guardian angel. To say that the angels always beheld the face of God meant that they had direct contact with God. Jesus is saying that, in God's sight, children are so precious that their guardian angels have the right of immediate access to the heavenly throne at all times. If this is so, we may confidently believe that the little one whose earthly life has ended is in the keeping of "Love Divine, all loves excelling." Even now, God is doing all that perfect love can do for the one so greatly loved.

In Matthew 18:44, there is the wonderful assurance that "it is not the will of my Father who is in heaven that one of these little ones should perish." Just as a normal human parent would never permit a child to be lost, so will our heavenly Father guard and guide the life now continuing beyond our sight. Our blessed Lord has not told us any details of heaven, but he did tell us that he will be there, and where he is, all will be well. All *is* well with dear Martha now in his near presence. The child of so much love, for whom so many prayers have been offered, who is of supreme value to our Lord and heavenly Father, is safe and safe forever. She may not come to us but we may go to her. Be not anxious about your dear child, John and Helen, says the Lord of life and conqueror of death. Her angel is always in touch with God. Your heavenly Father will never let her go, or stumble, or be hurt. And God himself shall wipe away all tears from her eyes.

(Reprinted from "Through The Valley Of The Shadow," CSS Publishing Company, Inc., © 1976.)

5

Lean
On God

Joe Barone

Isaiah 40:3-11 (NRSV)

CALL TO WORSHIP
   "Ascribe to the Lord, O heavenly beings, ascribe to the Lord glory and strength. Ascribe to the Lord the glory of his name; worship the Lord in holy splendor" (Psalm 29:1-2).

INVOCATION
   Gracious God, we seek your presence and we need your comfort here today. As we come to you in grief and in sorrow, we acknowledge that you are God, the One above all other gods, the only one who can bring us peace today. Amen.

OBITUARY

OLD TESTAMENT LESSON   Psalm 23 and Isaiah 40:3-11

NEW TESTAMENT LESSON   Luke 4:16-21

THE LORD'S PRAYER

BRIEF MESSAGE   "Lean On God"
   This chapter from Isaiah begins "The Book of the Consolation of Israel." After Israel had spent a long time away from God, God now brings God's comfort to God's people.

28

This Scripture holds up the reality of life. "All people are grass," Isaiah says. "Their constancy is like the flower of the field. The grass withers and the flower fades when the breath of the Lord blows upon it...."

But the story doesn't end there. "The grass withers and the flower fades," Isaiah says, "but the word of our God will stand forever."

God is eternal. God walks with us and cares for us, this great passage says. Even in Christ's first words in Luke, we can see God's hope that those who are struggling with poverty, illness, and oppression might be set free.

There is almost always grief when we come to the graveside, but there is hope, too. The hope is that God is here to hold us up. The hope is that God is like a shepherd who will lead us and help us find our way.

Because God is faithful, the path will be made more level, and the glory of the Lord will be revealed.

"Then the glory of the Lord shall be revealed, and all people shall see it together, for the mouth of the Lord has spoken," Isaiah says.

I know that our friend _____ was not a religious person, really, and he wouldn't want me to claim for him what he would not claim for himself.

But I also know that God is the God of all peoples, that God is a God of caring and of love, that God is the God who gently cradles us as would a loving mother. And so today, even in the grief we feel, we can lean on God.

Lift up your voice and do not fear, Isaiah tells the nations, and that's what I hear him telling me today.

Let us pray: Caring and Loving God, we thank you for the life of our friend _____, and for all our memories of him. We thank you also for the words God gives us through Isaiah. Help us hear those words and look to you for courage in the days to come. You and you alone are God, and you and you alone are worthy of our adoration. May we go forth from this place praising you. Amen.

PRAYER OF COMMITTAL

Gracious God, as we commit our friend _____ to you, we remember these words from the Psalms: "I will sing of your steadfast love, O Lord, forever; with my mouth I will proclaim your faithfulness to all generations. I declare that your steadfast love is established forever; your faithfulness is as firm as the heavens" (Psalm 89:1-2).

CLOSING PRAYER

Creator, Redeemer, Bringer of All Hope, we thank you for the friends and family who have gathered in this place today. We thank you for your love and for your faithfulness to us. We thank you for the strength you give us and for the courage you provide us. Walk with us and touch us with your peace in all the days to come. In Jesus' name we pray. Amen.

BENEDICTION

"Lord, [we leave this place reminded that] you have been our dwelling place in all generations. Before the mountains were brought forth, or ever you had formed the earth and the world, from everlasting to everlasting you are God" (Psalm 90:1-2).

Joe Barone is pastor of The First Christian Church (Disciples of Christ), Carrollton, Missouri.

6

God
Provides

Joe Barone

Matthew 14:13-21 (NRSV)

CALL TO WORSHIP

Hear these words from the Psalms: "I will give thanks to the Lord with my whole heart; I will tell of all your wonderful deeds. I will be glad and exult in you; I will sing praise to your name, O Most High" (Psalm 9:1-2).

INVOCATION

Gracious God, we thank you for this chance to worship you and to remember the life of _____. We come to this place knowing that you and you alone are God and so we must depend on you. You are the creator, the redeemer, the one who gives hope. Give us hope today. In Jesus' name we pray. Amen.

OBITUARY

OLD TESTAMENT LESSON   Psalm 23

NEW TESTAMENT LESSON   Matthew 14:13-21

THE LORD'S PRAYER

31

BRIEF MESSAGE   "God Provides"

As we come to bury _____ here today, we come in the presence of a loving God. That's the message that I want to bring. I didn't know _____, and I didn't have much chance to talk with his family, but I do know that God provides.

The Scripture from Matthew is one from the regular lectionary. It might seem to be an odd Scripture to use at a funeral, but if you stop and think about it, this Scripture, too, tells us that God provides.

Jesus took just a few loaves and fishes and turned them into enough to feed 5,000 people. He cared for those people, and he was unwilling to let them go away hungry.

He took the small gift of an unnamed giver, and turned it into plenty.

He took the skepticism of his own followers — "We have nothing here but five loaves and two fish," they told him — and he proved again that when human comfort and provision fail, God's comfort comes to touch us and to hold us.

This is the same Jesus who lived and died for us, the same Jesus who reflects God's everlasting love for every one of us. We may be grieving here today, but we grieve in the sure and certain knowledge that God will provide for us, even in our grief.

We come today to say good-bye to a friend and relative, but we come in the presence of God who cares for us and God's son who tells us over and over again — in both words and actions — that God does provide even beyond what we as human beings have the strength and power to understand until it happens.

"And all [of them] ate and were filled," the Scripture says of those who had been hungry. So it is with us. We can take our hopes and grief to God, and God will provide. God will provide.

Let us pray: Gracious and loving God, we thank you for the memories we have of _____. We thank you that you provide for us in all the things we have to face. We thank you for the promise of the Scripture, and most of all for your love which we see most perfectly in Jesus.

As Jesus took the loaves and fed the hungry, so may you feed us with the message of your comfort and your love. And as Jesus walked with his disciples in their lives and then beyond, so may you walk with us both now and always. In Jesus' name we pray. Amen.

PRAYER OF COMMITTAL

Almighty God, as we commit our friend _____ to you, we trust in your promises and we sing with the psalmist: "The Lord is my light and my salvation; whom shall I fear? The Lord is the stronghold of my life; of whom shall I be afraid?" (Psalm 27:1).

CLOSING PRAYER

Creator, Redeemer, Spirit of Life, we leave this place trusting in you. Walk with us and bring us your peace so that we can live in you both now and always. In Jesus' name we pray. Amen.

BENEDICTION

As we leave this place, let us hear again the words of our Lord Jesus Christ: "Peace I leave with you; my peace I give to you; not as the world gives do I give to you. Let not your hearts be troubled, neither let them be afraid" (John 14:27, RSV).

Go in peace! Amen.

Joe Barone is pastor of The First Christian Church (Disciples of Christ), Carrollton, Missouri.

7

The Predictables Of Life
In The Midst Of Death

James W. Robinson

Life is an unpredictable affair. Our highest hopes, most cherished dreams, our fondest ambitions, our best laid plans may be shattered and scattered by the changing tides of tomorrow. Tomorrow's tides may end a friendship, break up a love affair, or sweep the person dearest to us through the doors of death. Who knows? Tomorrow may be your last day on earth. Or mine.

It would be easy for us to become pessimistic and cynical because of life's unpredictables, if it were not for the fact that life holds some great certainties, too. When tomorrow tumbles down upon our heads and threatens to crush us, the great certainties of life enable us to survive disaster. They help us not merely to survive; they make us better and stronger persons. Let me mention just two of the things of which we may be certain in time of trouble.

The first of these certainties is this: When trouble comes we always discover that there is a multitude of those who care, composed of people who are touched by our tragedy and want to do all they can to be of help.

A flood covers most of nearby Bound Brook. A group of children stop curious spectators driving by in their cars, ask them for money to help flood victims, and, as a result, a massive community relief drive is started.

A house is levelled by fire. A family is left without food, shelter, and clothing. Neighbors pitch in to help, the newspapers pick up the story, and soon the family is back on its feet, thanks to many who really cared.

Death carries off someone we love. It happens unexpectedly. One day he is alive, sitting under a grape arbor, talking about his plans for tomorrow. That night, he is called by his Maker. First we are stunned; shock deadens the blow. Then the anesthesia of shock wears off and we begin to feel the awful hurt and heartache of bereavement. We would fall apart if it were not for the presence of those who care: mother, dad, children, sisters, brothers, friends, neighbors. They come quickly to take us in their arms and breathe comfort in our ears. Remember, too, that there are many people whom we do not even know — strangers — who read or hear of our bereavement and lift prayers to God in our behalf.

God is the second certainty I wish to mention. We may be sure of this: We are never out of sight or reach of One who loves us with a love that tongue nor pen can ever tell.

I am reminded of a chorus we used to sing at a summer church camp:

Wide, wide as the ocean, High as the heavens above,
Deep, deep as the deepest sea, Is my Savior's love.
I, though so unworthy, Still am a child of his care,
For his Word teaches me That his love reaches me, every-
where.

Let me assure you of this about God's love. I am speaking now chiefly for those closest to Harry.

• God will see you through these first difficult days of Harry's departure.

• God will help erase from your mind all but the best memories of the days you shared together.

• God will remove the cutting edge of grief and help you bear the dull pain of your loss, although it will never leave you completely.

• God will substitute his presence for Harry's until you meet him again.

• God wants to use this time of distress to bring Harry's family closer than they have ever been before.

• God has provided for life to go on in a Land of Never-Ending Light that lies beyond the valley of the shadow of death.

35

In that land of Eternal Light, relationships that were interrupted by death will be restored. Families will be reunited, differences will be patched up, and they will live together in perfect love and peace. They will know unbroken happiness and joy, because former pain and tears will have passed away forever.

Believing this, we may in confidence say, "Lord, into thy hands we commend the spirit of Harry."

Lord, take our hand, and help us to live in such a way that one day we may deserve to step into a blessed eternity, too.

(Reprinted from "The Beauty Of Being Prepared," by James W. Robinson, CSS Publishing Company., Inc., © 1982.)

for a young war veteran who died in a motorcycle accident near his home

8

God's
Wonderful Plans

Frank L. Starkey

Sometimes death comes suddenly and unexpectedly. In the midst of life, with every joy of living near at hand, the one we love is taken from us. The tragic events of life remind us of the death of those words uttered by the young man, David, long ago: Death is, indeed, but a step away.

We are grateful for the life of our son in the faith, Duane. He just returned, not many weeks ago, from serving our country in a foreign land, there in our behalf, to help ensure the freedom that we hold as a Christian principle, for all people. He served for you and me, for God and country.

That makes it doubly hard for us to see such a tragic event happen here in the safety of our own land and community. And yet, this, too, is a fact of life that we must face. How shall we understand it?

To do so, we must review some of the basic tenets of our Christian faith. God has created us out of love. And such a love, which we aren't really able to understand, carries with it certain dangers. Because God loves us, he must allow certain freedoms to operate. He must give us the chance to respond out of free choice to all we do. He refuses to make us behave in any certain, given way. We must be able to reject him as well as accept his love and care.

That means that he must then create all things with that in mind. And so he created certain basic laws to govern his creation, laws which make all sorts of mistakes and dangers possible, mistakes in good judgment, evil intentions, and the hazard of the other people around us as well.

And so it is, in that kind of an atmosphere, he shows us his love, and gives us an opportunity to grow in a real, joyous way.

But then you see how all sorts of misfortunes and evils can happen, too. Tragedies are possible every moment of every day. And so David said so very wisely, "Death is but a step away from any of us."

And yet, what a joy it is to know a good son. That is part of our created freedom, too. God has given us the joy of sharing in his creation through the giving of life to a son. He has given us the joy of watching that personality grow, of giving of our love to him, of sacrificing for his good, of knowing the same kind of relationship with our child as God has with us. As we go through the joys and sorrows of helping our children to grow, so God goes through the joys and sorrows of helping us to grow, in freedom — freedom to accept or reject his love.

If we were to leave our analysis here, it would be only selfish, for certainly our sorrow is for our own personal loss, and that's all right, too. It's right that we should know that personal sorrow.

But the overwhelming truth of the matter is that such a God, who is so great a God to allow all the freedoms he does, and to give us such a marvelous gift of life that he has, such a God does not leave us out in the cold because of tragedy. He has built into us the desire to preserve life with every ounce of know-how that he gives us. But, knowing how great our God is, we also know that, through the tragedies of life, he will never for a moment forsake us or our loved one. We can rest assured that he sees us through the valley of the shadow of death.

And all we have to do is look at all the things he has told us in his marvelous Word. Everything he did while he was here on this earth speaks to us of the assurance of the truth that we believe in. This is why we say Jesus is the Way, the Truth, and the Life. He didn't tell us about it; he demonstrated it always. He demonstrated his power over nature, mind, and body. He sealed it with his own resurrection. And he promised he would always be with us to be our source of strength.

And that power is still a reality for us today. Our experience of tragedy and loss is still the same. Our tears flow just as easily even after knowing this. But the Christ is still with us, and we face the time of sorrow in the strength that we receive from faith in him.

There are only three incidents recorded in the Scriptures of Jesus raising someone from the dead. Jesus couldn't go around doing this all the time. In fact, all these did finally die again. But you see the whole purpose was to tell us the truth of the fact that he is God; and God is love; so he created; and he will raise us again as he has promised. He overcomes our grief, for he reminds us that death is not an ending to existence, but rather the beginning of a new kind of life. "Eye hath not seen, ear hath not heard, what wonderful things God has planned for those who love him."

(Reprinted from "Through The Valley Of The Shadow," CSS Publishing Company, Inc., © 1976.)

9

Finding
Support

Elizabeth E. Conroy

Ecclesiastes 3:1-8　　**Psalm 129**
Romans 8:31-39　　**John 14:1-14**

I don't think that any of us are ever truly ready to say good-bye to a loved one. No matter how it happens, suddenly as the result of a car accident, or, as it was for Diane, slowly as a result of an illness, we wish we could have held onto our loved one just a little bit longer. Even when we see death as a friend who brings an end to pain and suffering, there is still something in us that wishes it had all been a bad dream — that our loved one had never taken ill and that life could go back to normal. Ron, Amy, and Marty, you will probably understand what I mean when I say that it is one of life's ironies that even as we rejoice that Diane is now free of pain and cancer and is enjoying eternal life we also long to have her healthy and well, with all her energy, back in this life. Our longing leaves us tired — aching inside from our grief.

Ron, I know from talking with Diane that there was so much life left that she wanted to experience with you. Diane wanted to keep on enjoying that special closeness that you rediscovered at the Marriage Encounter Weekend you were part of this year. Amy and Marty, your mom wanted to see graduations and celebrate at weddings and cuddle any future grandchildren. You have a special family — you enjoy a closeness that allows you to keep on loving each other even when you don't always like what the other person is doing. Diane didn't want to die — didn't want to be seen as giving up — didn't want to leave this life because she had so much living that she still wanted to do. She wanted more Christmas dinners at her parents with all her family, wanted more nights of coffee and talking with her friends, more competitions and chorus rehearsals, wanted to spend more time in her garden. Diane wasn't ready to give up on life but she understood, even as she wondered why she couldn't beat the cancer, that it would soon be her time to die.

I believe that Diane's understanding of her own death is expressed very well in today's Old Testament Lesson from Ecclesiastes. As the lesson points out there is a time for everything. There is a time to laugh and a time to cry, a time to sow and a time to reap, a time to build up and a time to tear down, and there is a time to be born and a time to die. That is the cycle of life. Ron, Amy, and Marty, you know that cycle for yourselves. You saw it as you watched Diane at work in her garden. In God's creation there is a time for everything. We are given the gift of human life by God and at the end of this life there is yet another gift from God — the gift of eternal life.

In the Gospel Lesson from John we hear Jesus' promise that he will prepare an eternal home for us. In Saint Paul's words from Romans we hear that if we have faith in Jesus Christ, if we have faith in the one who died on the cross so that our sins could be forgiven, then we also will enjoy eternal life with him. When Diane first asked me, over two years ago, if I would conduct her funeral I asked her if she wanted a Christian Service or a Memorial Service. For a moment, she looked surprised by my question, and then she said, "A Christian funeral. I believe in all of that even if I don't always go to church or don't always talk about it." I believe that because Diane had faith in our Lord Jesus Christ that she is right now enjoying that gift of eternal life, and if there really is such a thing as a barbershop chorus, then she's already passed the auditions and is singing her heart out.

Diane also knew and appreciated the beauty of God's creation. She knew what the psalmist meant when he said, "I will lift my eyes to the hills." Diane loved the earth, especially her garden.

41

Diane eagerly awaited the first robins in the spring and liked watching the Canada geese. Maybe she liked to hear their honking as they flew overhead, and maybe she admired their symmetry as they flew in their "V" formation.

Over the years, one of the poems Diane and I discussed together was written about Canada geese. This poem pointed out that Canada geese instinctively know that they can fly farther and with less effort by flying together, in formation, than they can if they fly individually. They know that they can get there more easily and faster if they fly in formation, and so they do it. They've learned that one goose on its own meets more resistance and tires too quickly. Geese have learned that they need encouragement from behind to strengthen them for what lies ahead. They have also learned that when one is hurting, it needs support, not just for a limited time but until that goose dies or until it is well enough to fly.

I know it can be dangerous to make too many comparisons between how the geese relate to each other and how we live, but I'm going to anyway because I am awed at all the geese have to teach us about dealing with our grief and living life fully. Each of us is here today because we have been touched, in some way, by Diane's death. We share something in common. We know what it means to experience loss. We know what it feels like to hurt inside. Each of us deals with our grief in our own way. There is no one right way to deal with the death of a loved one. There is no time limit placed on how long we grieve. Coming to terms is a solitary, personal experience but it need not be a journey we make alone. That's where the geese come in.

Think of geese. Each goose has to flap its wings for itself, but instinctively they knew that if they flew in formation, they'd fly farther, faster. We have to do our own grieving, but our grieving can be made easier if we take advantage of the people and the resources around us.

No matter how hard we try to cope on our own, there will be times we need to talk to others. There will be times when we need to know that someone else understands what we're going through — times when we need the encouragement of the voice, honking behind us, reminding us that what we're feeling is okay, telling us that we are loved, encouraging us so that we can deal with our grief. Ron, you and your family will be able to discover that kind of support amongst your family and friends. You will find that kind of support, should you choose to do so, with a church family, through one of the many bereavement groups which meet on a regular basis within our communities, through Diane's family and friends. You have to do your own grieving, but you can be helped through this process by the choices you make along the way.

There's yet another lesson to be learned from the geese. When a goose is hurting, it falls out until it is able to fly again. There is no time limit on how long it needs to heal. It simply takes all the time necessary. It is so easy for us to say to ourselves, "Well, that's silly. I should be over this by now." Be good to yourself. Don't deny your grief. Say, "This is how I'm feeling right now and that's okay." Allow yourself to grieve and enable yourself to heal.

If you are one of the geese that stays back to help and protect during the healing process, then the geese also have a message for you. Your support isn't for one week, or even one month. Your support is needed until the healing is complete — however long that takes. You are needed to help your friend or relative bear the burden they are carrying.

One of the many cards Diane received and saved read, "Have faith, God watches over you, He has you in his care. Have hope, for He is always near to hear your every prayer. Have trust that always, come what may, He'll help to see you through." Ron, Marty, and Amy, I pray that you and all of Diane's family and friends will be able to share in the same faith, hope, and trust in God that Diane held, so that you too may one day enjoy eternal life. May God's healing presence and peace carry you through the difficult days to come. Amen.

Ordained in 1989, Elizabeth E. Conroy is the pastor of Trinity Lutheran Church, Walkerton, Ontario.

10

We Remember
And Anticipate

Michael B. Brown

Psalm 23 (KJV)
John 14:1-1-6 (KJV)

We gather in this place on this day for a service of memory and anticipation. We remember the life of a loved one and the promises of God. And we anticipate the fulfillment of those promises in the life of her whom we mourn and in our own lives as well.

_____ was a wife, mother, and cherished friend. She was a person who across many years gave of herself for the sake of others, loving, teaching, and nurturing at home, in the community, and the church. One here remembers her as a life partner, a woman who shared his hopes and dreams, who joined with him in the parenting of three beautiful children, and who enhanced his understanding of the meaning of grace.

Three remember her as "Mom," one who changed their diapers, sang them lullabies, rocked them to sleep, chauffeured them to school functions, chaperoned their parties, ironed their shirts and dresses, fixed their meals, read them bedtime stories, and kissed their hurts away. In time she became for them the model of what it means to be an honest, hard-working, sensitive, Christian adult. Now, as long as they live in the memory of her witness, she will live through them.

Many remember her as a neighbor, friend, or church member. In every role she touched our lives with charm and wit, with courage

44

and hope, with kindness and faith. We at this church recall with gratitude the long hours of volunteer activity she rendered in countless activities, especially with older adult ministries. And we always knew her love for the church revealed a deeper love for the Lord of the Church.

Likewise, today we remember promises God made in both our scripture lessons. The first came from Psalm 23. "Yea, though I walk through the valley of the shadow of death, I will fear no evil, for thou art with me." Two important words are articulated there. First, we walk "through the valley of the shadow of death," not into it. We are not abandoned to our grief forevermore. Instead God will lead us through the pain to healing and wholeness on the other side. Second, "Thou art with me." As we face this time of mourning, there is an unseen Presence walking beside us. And we can lean on that Presence for comfort and counsel when otherwise we would fall. You are not alone in your grief. "I will fear no evil, for thou art with me."

Here's the other promise. In John 14, Jesus said to his disciples: "In my father's house are many rooms. If it were not so, would I have told you that I go to prepare a place for you? And if I go and prepare a place for you, I will return again and receive you unto myself, that wherever I am you may be also." What we call "death," Jesus calls "homecoming." There is a room in the Father's house, he said. It has been prepared by his own hands for your wife, for your mom, for our friend. Last week when you stood at a hospital bed, saying, "Good-bye," Jesus stood at the front door of the Father's house, saying, "Hello." In that promise we find our ultimate strength for facing this loss and all others like it: the promise of life beyond this life in a place where there is no sickness, no sadness, and no death. The risen Christ has made provisions for those whom he loves. And he loves your wife, your mother. And last week when you released her, his arms were open wide to embrace her.

Dr. Michael B. Brown is the senior minister of Central United Methodist Church, Asheville, North Carolina.

11

Reservations
For God's Children

Frank H. Seilhamer

Hebrews 11:13-16 (RSV)

> *These all died in faith, not having received what was promised, but having seen it and greeted it from afar, and having acknowledged that they were strangers and exiles on the earth. For people who speak thus make it clear that they are seeking a homeland. If they had been thinking of that land from which they had gone out, they would have had opportunity to return. But as it is, they desire a better country, that is, a heavenly one. Therefore God is not ashamed to be called their God, for he has prepared for them a city.*

In the novel *Roots* by Alexander Haley, Kunta Kinte, fresh off the ship that had brought him to America from Africa, is being whipped into line by his slaveowners. To break his spirit and make him compliant, the overseer gives him a new name, Toby, and tries to make him acknowledge that he is now part of the property of the plantation to which he has been dragged in chains.

He refuses to accept what he is told and is beaten into unconsciousness. The black man who is cleaning his wounds tries to give him advice about how to stay alive. *"You is Toby. And this is your home* now." *"No!"* he replies. "I may be *here now*, but *this* is *not* my *home*."

Though he had never heard of it, Kunta Kinte would have understood what the writer of the Epistle to the Hebrews was trying to convey when he wrote to the first century church about what it means to be strangers and exiles on earth, a part of the long line of God's people who were "here now" on earth, but who understood that they were not "at home."

Those figures of people on the road home, who with their tents on their backs have packed up and moved on to their "native land," were with me when I stood with Allean, Elaine, and Barry by Emory's bed last Wednesday night. I had sat near that very spot when I had visited him the previous Friday morning and given him communion. Weak as he was, but fully alert, Emory obviously was losing ground. I held his hand and said to him, "Are you afraid about what is happening to you?" "Afraid, no, but wish I could get it finished. This is taking too long. What I want is either to get strong enough to get up and go home, or (pointing to the ceiling) to get it over with and go home! I feel like a balloon with a slow leak. I know that even if I get to that first home, it won't be long before I go to the second one."

Neither of us could know that before another Friday arrived, he would step out of that bed onto the last leg of the road to that heavenly homestead he had in sight. God granted him time for goodbyes. The wife who had loved him and stood by his side for years and who nursed him through his long debilitating illness, the daughter and son who had been there when the need arose and who had him in as well as on their hearts were there for him in his final hours. They saw Emory off on the last leg of the journey we are all in the process of making. What comfort they gave him by being there to see him off so that he did not have to depart alone!

In human terminology that leave-taking is labeled *death*. That sticker, plastered on each instance of earthly departure, has for many the connotation of "perished." That aura surrounds the experience because we have been lured into believing a lie. That lie is this: that the earth is our home, and our time on it is the real, most vital stage of our existence. Birth is the starting blocks for our run on it, and death is the finish line of being.

Now, if the writer of Hebrews and Saint Paul are right, then seeing it that way is getting the ends of the issue reversed. The starting blocks for our life are the hands of God, and the finish line is coming full circle to fall against his breast.

What the Scriptures tell us is that existence is a continuum, a line that runs from point to point, with both ends in the hands of God. The part of that line which we travel along that stretches over this globe of ours is the shortest segment of our "string." The "earth leg" is a mere blip in our trek from our heavenly homestead on the way to return to it once more. What you and I so often call "life" is the learning phase of becoming the creatures God shaped lovingly in his hands. Death is the resting place where Emory, and eventually all of us, tuckered out by that interlude, step apart from all this planet's bustle to get rested for the final leg of the pilgrimage home.

Jesus used that image of death when he talked to the disciples the night when he was packing for his own earthly departure. After telling them about his death, he urged them not to misunderstand what was about to happen: "Let not your hearts be troubled; believe in God, believe also in me. In my Father's house are many rooms; if it were not so, would I have told you that I go to prepare a place for you? And when I go and prepare a place for you, I will come again and will take you to myself, that where I am you may be also" (John 14:1-3).

The word *rooms* is translated from the Greek word *mone*. A *mone* is a stopover, an oasis, along a caravan route, where travelers wearied and tattered from the trek can be revived, and have time to reflect on where they have been and where they are headed next! If that, indeed, is what death actually is, then "pilgrims" like Emory, who are on the move through "foreign" turf on their way "home," have nothing to fear from the stopover, nor have any of the ones who love them, who are left behind and awaiting their divine visas to "take off" on their departures to join him!

This "land of the living" is merely a place of "prelude"! We are routed through the earth, I suspect, to be given the chance to learn about love and growth, failure and pain, giving and sharing, meeting and parting, so that we can know what a glorious gift we are being given by God when we step beyond this "life" to one that has no end with him and each other. Life here and now, as part of that pilgrimage, should not be hastened, or squandered, as though it is nothing more than the lead-in to "the real thing"! But neither should it be clutched frantically as though it is all there is, or as if it is the place where our ultimate fulfillment, or security, or joy are to be found. For as "strangers and exiles on the earth ... we are seeking a homeland ..." designed for, and drawn toward "a better country," that is, "a heavenly one."

That is why we need to keep death's part of the pilgrimage in proper perspective, too. When we gather to say our good-byes to those who have died, who have struck their earthly tents and moved down the path that passes through the Valley of the Shadow, we must stay clear about who it is for whom we are grieving.

It surely cannot be for a pilgrim like Emory, who, loving the Lord and fixing his eyes on him since before he could remember, at this second is closer to "home" than we are! There is no reason to sorrow for him when it is to the One who "is not ashamed to be called their God," the One who is stretching eagerly to catch them up, toward whom he is running!

The fact is that the ones for whom we are grieving are the living, the people who loved him so much that they, as "pilgrims" and "strangers" themselves, are now struggling with getting on with the journey through this realm without him. It is for those still here, not for a dear friend and brother, that we grieve. Those who while still "here" are not at "home" are the ones who need our comfort! That is why it is to you, Allean, Barry, Elaine, and families, that we hold out our hands to console and lift up, showing you that we care. We have come together as friends. Here, hand-in-hand, seeing death as a stage on the road marked "Homeward Bound," we can nod our heads with Saint Paul: "If we live, we live to the Lord, and if we die, we die to the Lord; so then, whether we live or whether we die, we are the Lord's" (Romans 14:8, RSV).

And remembering that, even while we are still aching from our sense of separation, can help the most distraught "pilgrims" hang on to the divine promise that nothing, absolutely nothing, can separate Emory or us from that eternal home where God already has reservations made for all of his children!

Dr. Frank W. Seilhamer is currently Professor of Old Testament at Lutheran Bible Institute in California, Irvine.

12

Jesus' Grief And Yours

Charles J. Lopez, Jr.

Isaiah 61:1-3	John 14:1-6
Psalm 121	Matthew 11:28
John 11:21-27	Matthew 14:13-21

The Gospel Lesson is about the five loaves and two fish ... the familiar story of the feeding of the 5,000. It is a great story. Jesus had enough food to feed lots of people. We are glad when we hear the outcome of this story.

What we might miss at the beginning of this feeding text (Matthew 14:13-21, NRSV) is that Jesus is grieving over the recent death of his friend and cousin, John the Baptist. In fact, Jesus was so upset that Scripture tells us, "... he withdrew from there in a boat to a deserted place by himself...." Somehow the crowds found him and he did for the crowds what needed to be done — he fed them!

Like Jesus, we never know when death will come to a friend or loved one. We, too, are grief-stricken. We, too, need to be alone in a deserted place. We, too, need time to sort things out.

Sometimes death comes after long and hard struggles or when illnesses have taken their toll on bodies and minds. For Mildred, death came quickly. When death comes so quickly, we do not always know what to say, nor do we know what to do. We are caught off-guard. We feel alone, frightened, confused, and perhaps even angry. Not so long ago, Mildred was playing Uno® and laughing with church friends.

Death can be like a heavy burden. At times we, too, may feel weighed down with the surprise of death. Whatever the heavy burdens are, Jesus shares words of comfort and reassurance with us: "... come to me, all you who are weary and burdened, and I will give you rest" (Mark 11:28, NIV).

The journey of life has many surprises for each of us, and so, at times, we feel disappointed when something doesn't turn out as we had planned. Death always has a way of surprising us and shocking us. We may even be asking, "Why now?"

We could also say that we are never quite prepared. Yet the words from our Lord when John the Baptist was still alive and in prison serve as words of encouragement for all of us. They are words of promise for all of us. Jesus says, "Come to me ... and I will give you rest."

These words might surprise us. In fact, we might have thought that Jesus would have said something a bit more profound. However, in Jesus we do find rest ... and that, in and of itself, *is* profound. As the songwriter said, "Jesus is the lover of my soul!"

Our Lord watches out for us, even though we may find that difficult to accept today. We know that our Lord himself carried a heavy burden to the cross: it was the weight of our sin. Jesus felt alone and forsaken. Jesus died and rose triumphantly for you and for me.

Jesus tells us in John's gospel that there are many rooms in his Father's house. In fact, Mildred might just be visiting with Gladys Youngman in one of these rooms! Mildred always seemed to follow Gladys around anyway.

Furthermore, we know that Jesus is "the way, the truth, and the life" (John 14:6, NRSV) because he tells us so! We also know that without Jesus no one can go to the Father. Mildred knew these truths as well. She loved God and God loved her. Mildred was baptized, confirmed, and received holy communion from this altar many times. Mildred is God's child, so now she returns to God.

The psalmist says it best: "The Lord is your protector, and he won't go to sleep or let you stumble ... The Lord will protect you now and always wherever you go" (Psalm 121:3, 8). Mildred doesn't need her walker or cane anymore. She is not stumbling anymore. God is with her wherever she goes. In God's presence she is walking upright and straight! Thanks be to God for Mildred's life.

The peace of God which passes all understanding, keep your hearts and minds in Christ Jesus.

Hymns
"Beautiful Savior"
"Amazing Grace"
"How Great Thou Art"
"Joyful, Joyful, We Adore Thee"

Soloist
"Jesus, Lover Of My Soul"
"The Lord's Prayer"

Charles J. Lopez, Jr., Ph.D., is currently pastor of Grace Lutheran Church and Schools in Anaheim, California.

13

A Time To Be Born, A Time To Die

Charles J. Lopez, Jr.

Psalm 23   **John 14:1-6**
1 Corinthians 12:27—13:13   **Ecclesiastes 3:1-8**

The writer of Ecclesiastes reminds us that there is a time for everything. All time belongs to God — how well we know this today — for there is "a time to be born, and a time to die...."

We are here today because Marian was born, and now she has died. We give thanks to Almighty God for Marian's time with us, as a loving niece, sister, aunt, cousin, and friend.

We never know when death will come. So we all need to be ready to meet the Creator. Marian was ready! She loved the Lord and served him! Today is a victory celebration for Marian.

How do I know that Marian is celebrating with God? Because Marian shared her faith with me, as she said over and over again, "Pastor, I love the Lord!"

When Marian was baptized in North Dakota 85 years ago, the pastor made the sign of the cross on her forehead. She has been God's child ever since. Marian has been nurtured at the table for many, many years. One of her last requests to me as her pastor was to share holy communion with her. Even though she was very weak, she knew she wanted to taste the Lord's goodness one more time before leaving this world.

Now she is one of the *saints in glory,* now she is part of the *body of Christ,* now she is numbered among *the great cloud of witnesses,* and now *the foretaste of the feast to come* is with her!

53

We will have our moments of tears and we will be sorrowful and grieve. These are natural feelings for losing a sister and a good friend. But let us also rejoice with Marian, as she rejoices with the angels in heaven. Marian's suffering is over. She is breathing a lot easier. Marian is celebrating with God today!

The past several years were difficult for Marian. She had her good days and bad ones. Breathing and getting enough oxygen was the issue. Now Marian is able to breathe easier — for now the very breath of God is sustaining her. As Jesus promises in John's gospel, "I go to prepare a place for you ... for I am the way, and the truth, and the life!" Her room has been ready for a long time; now she takes her place among all the saints.

When I was with the family last Thursday, Marian pointed to me. She wanted Psalm 23 read out loud and she wanted to pray the Lord's Prayer. Marian loved the Lord and the Lord loved Marian. We at Grace Lutheran Church loved Marian and Marian loved the people at Grace Lutheran Church. Marian knew the Lord and she loved God's people. As the psalmist says, "He leads me beside still waters; he restores my soul ... surely goodness and mercy shall follow me all the days of my life, and I shall dwell in the house of the Lord forever!"

I encourage all of you to remember your stories of Marian. Share them among yourselves. This is really part of the healing process for all of us. There is a picture of Marian in the back of the church, right next to her sister Doris. One of the images I have of Marian and Doris is of them always being together. You were loving sisters. I remember Marian at our church picnics, oxygen and all, participating in everything that she was able. Marian was a part of our faith community and she will be missed. Marian was a leader in this faith community; she was a dedicated leader of the Women of the Church.

Rest assured that our Lord watches out for us. We know that our Lord himself carried a heavy burden to the cross: it was the weight of our sin. Marian's sin is gone. She now has the title of saint. We know that Jesus died for you and for me. Jesus died so that you and I can live with God forever in one of those rooms!

God's faithfulness is for eternity. There is a time for everything, "a time to weep, and a time to laugh; a time to mourn, and a time to dance ..." (Ecclesiastes 3:4, NRSV). Thanks be to God for Marian's life.

The peace of God which passes all understanding, keep your hearts and minds in Christ Jesus.

Apostles' Creed

Prayers

Hymns
    "Jesus, The Very Thought Of You"
    "Beneath The Cross Of Jesus"
    "I Love To Tell The Story"
    "Beautiful Savior"

Soloist
    "The Lord Is My Shepherd"
    "How Great Thou Art"

Charles J. Lopez, Jr., Ph.D., is currently pastor of Grace Lutheran Church and Schools in Anaheim, California.

14

Life's
Short Circuit

Lawrence H. Craig

Revelation 14:13 (RSV)

And I heard a voice from heaven saying, "Write this: Blessed are the dead who die in the Lord henceforth." "Blessed indeed," says the Spirit, "that they may rest from their labors, for their deeds follow them."

Blessed is _____, for he is now at rest from his labors: the labor of struggling with his recent illness, the labors of pulling wire and installing electrical outlets, the labors of serving his Lord in the church and being a distinguished Elder Emeritus. Without a doubt, _____'s many deeds follow him. We all shall miss our long trusted and dear friend, who in this life exemplified discipleship in Jesus Christ.

As family members you shall miss him, for _____ loved and dedicated his life to his wife, children, and grandchildren. You shall miss his craving for peanut butter on graham crackers. This church will miss _____'s enthusiastic, friendly smile, his special laugh, and his explanation of getting _____ home before 11:00 a.m. so he wouldn't get stuck with buying her lunch.

I shall miss his wisdom and presence and his labors of love when he was working in this building. _____ especially knew everything about the boiler, for he maintained it for years. I recall countless times when I phoned him because the building was cold. He always knew what switches to flip, what buttons to push, and what boxes to tap with a screwdriver handle. _____'s knowledge gave physical warmth to our building and bodies, yet much more significantly, _____'s love of life, his love of Christ, and his love for us always brought spiritual warmth to our hearts.

_____ was an electrician by trade. Why, there's no telling how many miles of wire _____ pulled in his life or how many rolls of black tape he used to provide for his family's needs. We have to admire electricians. Electricity is dangerous and a mysterious thing. It's hard to understand and powerful yet _____ knew all about it. He knew how to work with it to achieve its benefits. _____ knew about positive and negative leads. _____ knew the importance of having a good solid ground. _____ knew what it meant to make good connections when splicing wires together with wire nuts.

What is true of _____ in his electrical trade was equally true of _____ when it came to his faith and his life and leadership in the church. _____ always took a positive lead and kept the negatives in check. He showed us by example the importance of having our lives firmly grounded in the scriptures, the word of God. _____ knew a good connection was important for electrical power to benefit our lives. He also knew the value of having a good connection to God, through Jesus Christ, for spiritual well-being.

Electrical power enables us to be here on this bitter cold morning. When you turned your ignition key, electrical power started your car. Electrical power runs our world, provides heat and light for this sanctuary, and blesses our lives. Yet in life, once in a while, something happens. Once in a while something unexpected and unwanted occurs. A short circuit develops. Suddenly the car won't start, the boiler won't heat, and the lights don't cast off the darkness. _____'s death is one of life's short circuits. Your lives have been changed; they are different and don't seem right. And they're not. Where there was light, you now find darkness. Where there was warmth and joy, you now experience coldness and sorrow. Where power once flowed, such strength is now diminished. When a short circuit occurred in your homes and in this church, we called on _____. He would use his skills, repair the problem, and bring back the power for life to go on.

When we experience the death of those close to us, we must call upon God, as we do this morning. Turning to the scriptures, we learn of Christ's precious love and God's spiritual presence. The Good News is that God shall repair your brokenness, pain, and sorrow. God shall provide the ground you need to be firmly connected in your faith. God shall grant each of you comfort, healing, and hope in the days and weeks ahead of you. I place you in the trust and loving care of this God. Call upon God in prayer; seek God's presence in scripture; share God's comforting love as you love and care for one another. For God will repair the short circuits in your life. God will mend your brokenness. God will allow the power to surge once again in your life and you shall be a blessing to others, as _____ has been a blessing to each of us.

Lawrence H. Craig is pastor of St. Paul's United Church of Christ, Hermitage, Pennsylvania.

15

Fishing With
A Harmonica

Lawrence H. Craig

Matthew 4:18-20 (RSV)
*As he walked by the Sea of Galilee, he saw two broth-
ers, Simon who is called Peter and Andrew his
brother, casting a net into the sea; for they were fishermen. And he said to them, "Follow me, and I will
make you fishers of men." Immediately they left their
nets and followed him.*

Jesus said, "Follow me," and the fishermen followed him. Not
at day's end when their chores were over. Not at some later time
when they had absolutely nothing better to do. The fishermen followed Jesus, immediately! They were prompt in answering our
Lord's call. _____, as we all know, was one who followed
Jesus immediately. He was a dependable servant of God and a distinguished servant to his community. He, too, was prompt when
called upon to answer the Lord's call whenever and wherever that
call came to serve.

The story is told that _____ and a couple friends were
out fishing one day. Nothing was happening. The lines lay motion-
less on the water. The fish were not biting. The suggestion was
made that _____ play his harmonica. Like a shiny new
lure, out of his pocket it came. Music filled the air. Even the fish
were moved, for as _____ played, two fish were caught.

Personally, I don't believe I would want to fish with a harmonica. For one, I can't play a harmonica and any effort, even my best, would totally disrupt with screeching the peace and serenity nature intends to offer us. Secondly, I was always taught that you had to remain still and quiet when you fished. I also was taught that once you put the line in the water, you had to whisper if you spoke anything at all. So in playing a harmonica, I can only envision bass and walleyes, crappies and muskies leaving the area quickly in great schools. Yet, _____ played a harmonica and the fish started to bite. So many people over the years were drawn to the specialness of this man we all knew as _____, just as those fish seemed drawn to _____'s music that day when he played his harmonica at the advice of friends.

Today we celebrate the life of _____, who gives us cause to rejoice over life and praise God continually. Jesus said to the fishermen, "Follow me, and I will make you fishers of men." When _____ heard those very words, like the first followers of our Lord, he immediately left what he was doing and followed Christ, fulfilling whatever task his faith and the needs of others led him to.

_____ lived his faith openly. A man of zest and energy, he was generous to all. He filled the world around him with the music of his harmonica and with the joyfulness of singing. With his talents he made furniture and crafts which he gave away. _____ planted and nurtured gardens. He walked woodlands and knew the wonderment of God in living life to its fullest. _____ appreciated life's many simple joys, one of which was his dog. _____ told me, when hospitalized, he was not afraid to die and shared openly his confident faith in our God.

In his hobby of gardening, _____ was a tiller of the soil and a planter of seeds. The apostle Paul says, "What you sow does not come to life unless it dies. And what you sow is not the body which is to be," for it will be changed. "What is sown is perishable, what is raised is imperishable. It is sown in dishonor, it is raised in glory. It is sown in weakness, it is raised in power. It is sown a physical body, it is raised a spiritual body" (1 Corinthians 15:36-37, 42-44, RSV). The apostle Paul, in these words, is emphasizing the tremendous hope we all have because of Christ's resurrection. Paul speaks directly to us about what occurs when we die. Because of _____'s faith, because of our faith, we are able to face the future unafraid, knowing that when death occurs we shall be changed and new life shall be ours.

Because this new life is a gracious gift of God, we are people of hope. This hope gives us strength in our weakness, comfort in our sorrow, confidence in our despair. God's new life and new light breaks through the pain and confusion and removes the darkness of death's shadow. _____ knew this and proclaimed it in the living of his days. We, too, know this through our faith and through Christ's example to us. This is the Good News we have been given to help us cope with the loss of this one we loved. This is the Good News that enables us to leave here today. Good News that proclaims the Spirit of God goes with us into the living of these days.

Lawrence H. Craig is pastor of St. Paul's United Church of Christ, Hermitage, Pennsylvania.

16

Jesus Called
To Her

T. A. Kantonen

Luke 13:12 (RSV)
And when Jesus saw her, he called her and said to her, "Woman, you are freed from your infirmity."

We have today a heartfelt sense of great loss. The family has lost a devoted wife and tender mother. The community has lost a leader whose competence and willingness could always be depended upon in every good enterprise. A vast circle of friends has lost a true and unselfish friend whose personality was radiant with understanding and sympathy. The church has lost not only a loyal member but also a talented and faithful worker who gave herself wholeheartedly to Christian service. Many of us are better because she was with us. We thank God for her and we bless her memory. God has spoken to us through her life and character. Today we wish to listen to what God speaks to us through her death.

The text of our meditation was selected many weeks ago when it became apparent that Helen would not recover, but that it was God's will to make her lingering illness the gateway into the life eternal. I had come to know her very well, and there is no other passage in the Word of God that I deem more fitting for this occasion.

Portrayed here is a scene from the latter days of our Lord's earthly ministry. He has entered a Galilean synagogue on a Sabbath day. As he looks over the congregation in the little church, his

62

eyes become fixed upon one of the worshipers. It is a woman who has suffered for a long time. As the months and the years went by and the illness persisted, her body gradually lost its upright posture and she became bent as though she carried an invisible heavy burden. But she came to the Lord's house faithfully just the same, for her heart was there. Then came the day when her faithfulness was gloriously rewarded. She looks up and before her is the Savior himself. His lips move and he speaks, not to the congregation in general, but to her personally. It is a healing and redeeming word that he speaks, such as only the Savior can speak. "And when Jesus saw her, he called her and said to her, 'Woman, you are freed from your infirmity.' While he speaks, his hand touches her and at once the binding shackles fall. She rises from her cramped posture, her body straight and strong, and she goes home praising God.

Against the background of this touching little story from the Bible, we think today of Helen. She, too, came faithfully to God's house and drew strength from his word. She, too, was given a heavy burden of suffering to bear through long weary days and nights which seemed never to end, a burden which strained every ounce of her endurance almost to the breaking point. Loving hands ministered to her, it is true, and everything within human reach was sought to alleviate the suffering. But the crushing burden was still there, to be borne day after day, week after week, month after month. Like her Master, as he writhed in the bitter agony of the cross, she, too, was forced to look up into the face of God and cry, "My God, why?"

To find the answer, she and her pastor were compelled to explore deeply the mysterious ways of God. Does not the Bible tell us that Christ himself was made perfect through suffering? He could not be the Savior that he is and enter so deeply into our sorrows had he not been subjected to such pain and agony of his own. When the divine Craftsman holds us to the wheel of pain and the flames of suffering, when the chisel of agony stabs us, should we not press our lips together and not whimper, for is this not God's way of fashioning a more Christ-like character? Does not the very fact of suffering show that there is something in us that is precious to God? Otherwise, he would not spend so much time and take so much care with us, as he puts us through the purifying and refining process. Can there be any genuine courage or sympathy or unselfishness without suffering? And when foundations are being dug very deep, is it not because a great and high structure is in the making?

These were some of the answers that God gave us. But the great lesson was to learn to trust God even when we could not understand his ways. More than once she found comfort in that faith of which the poet sang:

> *Not till the loom is silent*
> *And the shuttles cease to fly,*
> *Shall God unroll the canvas*
> *And explain the reason why*
> *The dark threads are as needful*
> *In the weaver's skillful hand,*
> *As the threads of gold and silver*
> *In the pattern he has planned.*

It was this faith that ripened into a quiet sustaining assurance as the sunset gradually passed and the shadows of night began to fall. Prayer became more and more fervent and Heaven more and more desirable. Faith lifted the clouds of pain and allowed God's love to shine through. Like the woman of our text, she looked to her Lord alone for the deliverance which no power on earth could bring. Resting upon the everlasting arms, she was concerned at the end not so much about herself as about others, anxious only about the worry and discomfort which her condition was causing to her loved ones.

At long last came the hour of deliverance. The Savior's eyes sought her out from our midst, his redeeming hand was placed upon her, and his lips spoke the liberating word, "Helen, you are freed from your infirmity; you have waited long enough; you are very tired; you have done your day's work; I will give you rest."

On my last pastoral visit, she could no longer open her eyes to see me or respond to my voice. A higher and better Pastor had taken charge. I could only commit her to his keeping with the beautiful words of the church's order for the commendation of the dying, "Depart in peace, thou ransomed soul."

To the bereaved, let me add this word of consolation. Helen's life and departure from this life preach a much better sermon than I could preach. We feel a sense of great loss, it is true, but we know that such a life is never lost. She has but entered another room in God's great house, where the Master of all good workmen has set her to work anew. She has been freed from infirmity to serve God in new strength and loveliness. And she continues to serve you, too, for her memory will inspire you to follow her and her Savior and to bind you closer to one another. Heaven will be all the more desirable to you because she has gone there before you. And so we do not sorrow as those who have no hope. We thank God for what he has given us through her and we pray:

Lord, Jesus, King of Paradise,
O keep us in thy love,
And guide us to that happy land
Of perfect rest above;
Where loyal hearts and true
Stand ever in the light,
All rapture through and through,
In God's most holy sight.

(Reprinted from "Through The Valley Of The Shadow," CSS Publishing Company, Inc., © 1976.)

17

Amazing Grace

James W. Robinson

Long before Florence became a charter member of this church, John Newton wrote a hymn that has remained among the leaders in the hit parade of Christian music. It has been around for nearly two centuries. Christians have sung it with shining faces and tear-dimmed eyes in little white country churches nestled in groves of trees and in great stone churches located in the heart of bustling cities. On occasion its lyrics and haunting melodic strains have held the unchurched youth of America enthralled.

I could not help but think of that hymn of timeless appeal when I stood in the hospital at Florence's bedside with her husband and daughter. We knew that Mother had only a few more hours to spend on this earth. It was a heartbreaking experience for all; but I heard nothing from either of her loved ones but words of praise for God's amazing grace.

Now grace in Christian usage simply means God's love. It means his care and kindness beyond anything that anyone deserves. Grace is God's unexpected love that comes to meet us at a turn in the road that we are afraid to take. Grace is God's love that comes to lift us up just at the moment we are ready to give up. Grace is God's love that throws forgiving arms around us when we have sinned and least deserve his favor.

Florence would awaken to instant recognition of the meaning of the word "grace" if by some miracle she could hear us now. And perhaps she can. She knew that God loved her, and she loved God in return. She showed her love for him by her faithfulness to the church. She demonstrated it by her devotion to her home and husband. She exemplified it in her very life. It was evident in her exhortations to her children in respect to their God, their church, their country, and their fellow humans. As a result, her influence will live for generations to come. "Blessed are the dead which die in the Lord from henceforth: Yea, saith the Spirit, that they may rest from their labors; and their works do follow them."

One verse of that great old hymn reads, in part, "Through many dangers, toils and snares, I have already come." Florence knew from firsthand experience all about the "dangers, toils, and snares" of life. They were part of daily existence. When Florence became a charter member of this church, the Great Depression was beginning to take its toll on the economy and affect every family. Children came along, six of them, one after another. There were sacrifices to be made, corners to be cut, pennies to be hoarded, so that she could put food on the table and clothes on her children's backs.

Then her sons went off to war. One, a flier, was shot down behind enemy lines. For ten horrible months she suffered unspeakable mental anguish, not knowing if he was dead or alive. Later, many years after his rescue, he was to die a premature death as a result of his ordeal.

Toward the end of her days, Florence, who had always led an active life, was confined to her home by a crippling disease. These thoughts and others have been passing through the minds of her husband and children during these past few difficult days.

I do not speak of these things to cause them greater sorrow. I mention them so that I may say this: Florence survived all "dangers, toils, and snares" with her faith intact. If we could hear her now, she would be saying, "It was grace that pulled me through: the loving care and kindness of my heavenly Father."

God's amazing grace is not given simply to muscle through the trials and tribulations of this life. God gives us his grace so that we can make it home. Home? What does that mean?

To the person who is not a believer, home is the hole at the end of the road, the final resting place. To the person who is a believer, home is that place or condition or state of being — call it what you will — beyond the grave where God comes to meet us after our eyes close in death.

When I stand at the grave of my son, I remember all too clearly the crack of the rifles of the honor guard, the sound of taps floating lazily over the cemetery to the nearby wooded hills. I know that his body is there; but I believe that he — himself — is with God.

So, too, has Florence gone to be with God. To behold the Father's face; to be in the fellowship of Christ; to be a guest of God awaiting your homecoming, family, a reunion you may enjoy if you keep the faith.

You who loved Florence can honor her memory best by believing in and trusting in God's amazing grace, as she did. Remember, grace is God's incredible love. Search your Bible to learn more of what it means and how wonderful it really is. Stay close to God in prayer to keep it alive and operative in your heart. Remember how it alone kept your loved one going through thick and thin.

If you will do those things, God will send comfort to replace the sorrow you now feel. He will send healing to take away your hurt. He will give you faith to overcome your doubt. He will come to your house himself to share your loneliness. And you will be gripped by the conviction that through amazing grace you will one day see your Father's face — and the face of your dearest Florence.

> *Amazing grace! How sweet the sound That saved a wretch like me!*
> *I once was lost, but now am found; Was blind, but now I see.*
> *'Twas grace that taught my heart to fear, And grace my fears relieved;*
> *How precious did that grace appear The hour I first believed!*
> *Through many dangers, toils, and snares I have already come;*
> *'Tis grace hath brought me safe thus far, And grace will lead me home.*
> *The Lord hath promised good to me, His word my hope secures;*

He will my shield and portion be, As long as life endures.
When we've been there ten thousand years, Bright shin-
ing as the sun,
We've no less days to sing God's praise Than when we'd
first begun.

— John Newton

(Reprinted from "The Beauty Of Being Prepared," by James
W. Robinson, CSS Publishing Company, Inc., © 1982.)

for a church member who suffered a heart attack

18

The
Victory

Robert S. Kinsey

On that first Easter morning, three women were hurrying through the dark, narrow streets of Jerusalem. According to God's plan on that first Easter, the sun was destined to rise on the greatest day in history. No, the women did not carry brightly colored pocketbooks on that first Easter, nor did they wear bright colors. Weren't they in mourning? Didn't they have a sad and solemn duty to perform? They were not hurrying to greet a risen Savior; they were going to anoint a corpse, a corpse buried in a borrowed tomb on Good Friday. One question dominated their thinking: "Who will roll away the stone for us from the entrance to the tomb?" (Mark 16:3). You know the outcome of this event which began in sorrow and ended in joy. The stone was rolled away. There was no corpse to anoint. They listened to the greatest — and probably the shortest — Easter sermon ever preached. A sermon preached not by a seminary graduate but by an angel from the eternal heavens: "Don't be alarmed," he said. "You are looking for Jesus of Nazareth who was nailed to the cross. But he is not here — he has risen! Look, here is the place where they laid him...."

You and I love and worship and serve the Risen Lord. Because he lives, our loved ones shall live. He has overcome sin, death, and the grave. Wasn't the first item on the agenda of the early church to proclaim the resurrection of God's Son? Up and down the Mediterranean world they went, not with a Bible under their arms, but with the message of the Risen Savior in their hearts and on their lips. *Jesus Christ is alive.* He lives and reigns for all eternity. Because he lives, you and I shall live, and our loved ones whom we give over to his care will live!

To you, Bev, Barb, Gene, and the rest of the family, I say ... remember! Remember that death does not have the last word. No one can deny that death is an enemy. Doesn't God's book describe death as the last enemy to be overcome (1 Corinthians 15:26)? Remember, though, that death does not have the last word: the Word Incarnate has the final word, a word of victory and hope!

Today we honor the memory of Marshall E. Leiter, father, brother, grandfather, and friend ... a faithful member of Trinity Church. Recently Marshall returned to Ashland and joined again the church where his parents were so faithful and where Marshall had been baptized and confirmed by Dr. Arthur Smith. Marshall planned to come to one of the Holy Communion services last Sunday. Doesn't Holy Communion foreshadow that Messianic banquet in heaven when our Lord himself will be the host? In faith, we know that Marshall will be a guest at that banquet.

As we sit here in the presence of death, what do we learn? Life is short. Didn't Job say, "My days are swifter than a runner" (Job 9:25)? If Job were living today, he would probably say, "My days are swifter than a jet." Since life is short, shouldn't the prayer of the psalmist be on our lips, too: "So teach us to count our days that we may gain a wise heart" (Psalm 90:12, NRSV).

Marshall's death makes that other world even more real. Wasn't Henry Ward Beecher trying to express the same thought when he said, "Tears are often the telescope through which men see far into heaven"?

As a family, a time like this will bring you even closer together in your common sorrow. As you comfort each other and as you meditate on the ultimate issues of life, you will be inspired to minister to others who walk through the valley of sorrows.

On that first Easter morning, the women were sure that they had a sad and solemn duty to perform. They did not anoint a corpse; they learned about a Risen Savior — your Savior and mine. In faith we commit Marshall into Christ's loving care. Together with Paul we sing the victory song: "Where, O death, is your victory?

Where, O death, is your sting? ... But thanks be to God, who gives us the victory through our Lord Jesus Christ!" (1 Corinthians 15:55, 57, NRSV).

(Reprinted from "Through The Valley Of The Shadow," CSS Publishing Company, Inc., © 1976.)

19

When A
Christian Dies

Jerry L. Schmalenberger

Last Sunday, Mrs. Dwight (Roberta) Keller drove to her church for worship, as was her custom. She had for years helped in the nursery, took part in the church school, and faithfully worshiped as a part of our family of God.

She died while seated in the pew last Sunday during the sermon.

The ushers carried her out on a cot. I slipped out while Dr. Frank Seilhamer was preaching and had the "commendation of the dying" for her — right behind this altar. We held her funeral Wednesday here, right where she died. Her pall-covered casket sat there in the aisle with the paschal candle light shining upon it. Because that death was a shock, a hurt, and yet such a beautiful thing, we who are a part of her family of God must talk about it today. There were some great lessons acted out right in this place last Sunday and I want to remind you of them.

Our worship here is more than words — there are *grave* implications in all we do around this altar. Roberta Keller's death in our midst was one of God's visual aids. Think of the words she said before she died:

In *her confession* ... "increase in us true knowledge of thee and of thy will, and true obedience to thy word, that by thy grace we may come to everlasting life; through Jesus Christ our Lord."

I promised her in the absolution — "He (she) that believeth, and is baptized, shall be saved."

I stepped to the altar and read the Introit from the Psalm: "The sorrows of death compass me ... in my distress I called upon the Lord: and he heard my voice out of his temple: the Lord is my rock and my fortress."

I prayed in the *collect*, "Oh, Lord, we beseech thee favorably to hear the prayers of thy people that we, who are justly punished for our offenses, may be mercifully delivered by thy goodness...."

In the *creed,* she joined me in stating our belief about death: "I believe in the Holy Ghost; the Holy Christian Church, the communion of Saints; the forgiveness of sins; the resurrection of the body, and the life everlasting."

In the *Peace* — another member got up and went over to her and extended her hand in friendship, "The peace of the Lord be with you" — "And with you also!" — the last words she said.

Then came the sermon hymn. I had selected it because it talked about the ministry. But verse two said, "As laborers in thy vineyard, Lord, send them out to be content to bear thy burden of weary days for thee; to ask no other wages when thou shalt call them home, but to have shared the travail which make thy kingdom come."

And then she died — the last sound from her throat a hymn to her God. Certainly, in this context, this perspective, we see the preciousness of the things we do called worship. When we come together to worship and study, it's more than another service club — more than enjoying each other's fellowship. Certainly more than a good or bad anthem or sermon. We begin our relationship with God at this font. We deal with things eternal and not only life here but also beyond the grave. How can some say it is old fashioned? How can some cry "irrelevant"? How can any parent claim to let their children decide for themselves?

Certainly more important than home, nation, job, marriage partner, or income, not just a temporary fad or just a good feeling, we are far more than a nice organization that does kind things. We do more than have a moment of silence for the deceased. We handle here the equipment and tools of salvation.

On April 5, 1913, the Rev. Simon Peter Long baptized an infant at this very baptismal font by the name of Roberta Pittinger.

Pastor Long pronounced this blessing: "Almighty God, the father of our Lord Jesus Christ, who hath begotten thee again of water and the Holy Ghost, and hath forgiven thee all thy sins, strengthen thee with his grace unto life everlasting." That prayer with that gift was answered last Sunday morning for Roberta Keller. That brings me to the second lesson.

We have a gift to give. What a beautiful thing it is that Mrs. William Lantz got up and went over to extend "the Peace" to Mrs. Keller, who was by herself. We never know what it may mean when we do an act of kindness like that. Let's promise ourselves right now we'll not wait until someone dies to do the nice things. Let's promise we'll put it off no longer, that we'll take the first step, that we'll make the first move, that we'll extend our hand, too, and give God's peace to all of the lonely, or stubborn, or comfortable, within our reach. It won't be necessary to send flowers when they die, because they'll know how we treated them when they lived.

The Contac commercial on television used to say: "Give your hand to a friend and give your heart to your love, but give your cold to Contac." We Christians put it: "Give your hand to a friend, give your heart to your love, and give your life to Jesus Christ."

There are always in our worship service some who will never be back. They die; we die; everyone dies. There are those who try this worship once and decide on that basis whether they'll ever return again. There are always opportunities for us to extend our hand in kind friendship. We always have the opportunity to encourage, to bless, to strengthen, and to give hope. The peace that comes to the saved and the peace which passes all understanding and the peace of being "in Christ" and the peace we sing about at Christmas and sense after Easter — we pray for and give thanks for — it is ours and we extend it! That's quite a gift we have to give! Indeed, we have a gift to give.

Life is uncertain and our task urgent. The Scripture tells us: "In the midst of life we are in death." I'm especially reminded of this when called sometimes five times in a single week to go to the dying or comfort the grieving. You aren't reminded that often as a congregation. Now, by Roberta Keller dying right in your midst,

75

let it be a weighty reminder that life doesn't go on forever. We are not immune from accidents and poor health and all the other hazards of a sinful world. That great Psalm 90 begins: "Lord, thou hast been our dwelling place in all generations," and then continues, "... so teach us to number our days that we may apply our hearts unto wisdom" (KJV).

Suppose today was your last on this earth (and it might be). What would your last actions be? What would your last words contain? Would you have been peeved because of a church council decision or because you have been slighted by the pastor or the church was cold or you were critical because of something in the bulletin or something that was omitted from the bulletin? Would your last words be some kind of gossip during the processional hymn or prelude? Life is too short to hate and be critical. Life is too uncertain to drift away from the church which is God's family or to be angry with each other. Don't hang up your faith in silly little incidental matters which really aren't important to salvation anyway. Jesus urges us to be ready anytime with a hymn of praise on our lips and in communion with his disciples. Matthew recorded Jesus as saying, "So be prepared, for you don't know what day your Lord is coming. Just as a man can prevent trouble from thieves by keeping watch for them, so can you avoid trouble by always being ready for my unannounced return."

It is a wise provision that you don't know when it comes: "Watch therefore, for you know neither the day nor the hour."

Foreknowledge is withheld, but the memory is given. This way life is happier, activities more intense, plans are bigger and better than if we knew. But uncertainty ought to urge readiness and readiness for death should increase the joy of life. Life is uncertain and our task urgent!

Let's remind ourselves what we believe about the death of a Christian. We say it in our Creed (she said it, too): "The forgiveness of sins; the resurrection of the body and the life everlasting." Everyone must die because we are all sinners and the Old Testament tells us: "The soul that sins shall die." But we have a life after this earthly life is over and a new spiritual body promised to us and a resurrection like Jesus Christ. Paul writes: "The fact is that Christ did actually rise from the dead, and has become the first of millions who will come back to life again some day" (1 Corinthians 15:20, TLB). The Living Bible puts it like this: "Everyone dies because all of us are related to Adam, being members of his sinful race and wherever there is sin, death results. But all who are related to Christ will rise again" (1 Corinthians 15:22). For us who have the power to become the sons of God, death is just a process — we go *through* the valley of death to life beyond.

For those we leave behind, it is a sad experience, but not so for the one who dies. We Christians get together on the morning of the first day of the week because of what Jesus Christ did on that day. Easter — we pack our churches and we sing, "Hallelujah, he is risen" and "Jesus Christ is risen today." Saint Paul promises us that Jesus' resurrection was the first one and we have one, too. Paul puts it, "How we thank God for all this! It is he who makes us victorious through Jesus Christ, our Lord!" (1 Corinthians 15:57, TLB). So, last Sunday, while we gathered to celebrate the Good News — that everyone of us has an Easter, too — Roberta Keller died. We could very well sing today, "Hallelujah, *she* is risen," or "Roberta Keller is risen today, Hallelujah."

Paul wrote to a little group in Corinth that doubted the resurrection this blunt statement: "For if there is no resurrection of the dead, then Christ must still be dead. And if he is still dead, then all our preaching is useless and your trust in God is empty, worthless, hopeless ... and you are very foolish to keep on trusting God to save you." He added: "And if being a Christian is of value to us only now in this life, we are the most miserable of creatures" (1 Corinthians 15: 13-14, 17, 19, TLB).

Yet one more lesson from Mrs. Keller's death here in God's house — we are the communion of the saints. That means the family or fellowship of the saved. Through our baptism we received that priceless gift of complete forgiveness and were adopted by God as his own children. We have the benefits of what Jesus did on that cross. We wear crosses, hang one over the altar, rotate one on our steeple, put them on our lapels, get blessed by their sign. All this to remind us of how important it is and that we have its benefits.

Don't mumble it — don't say it with a half yawn on your face — don't let your mind drift when we get to that part of the Creed: "The Holy Christian church, the communion of saints; the forgiveness of sins; the resurrection of the body and the life everlasting."

It took an unusual birth in Bethlehem, a rugged childhood in Nazareth, three long years of Pharisees' and Sadducees' criticism, the betrayal of a partner, the denial of a close friend, the ridicule of the religious, the distrust of his own family, the cruelty of the mock trial, the sweating of blood, and nails driven through his hands. It took agony of thirst, excruciating pains of crucifixion, and the blasting wide open the doors of the tomb. God invested a lot of himself in that plan — that also we might say it every first day of the week: "The communion of saints, the forgiveness of sins; the resurrection of the body and the life everlasting." Don't mumble those words.

We are the communion (fellowship) of saints. We are the saved who have had the sacrifice. In this faith we have (and give) comfort. So each time we come together and worship and commune, we join with all those baptized who have died before us and all those baptized in the world worshiping today and all the unborn saints yet to be his. Mrs. Keller worships with us today and so do all the rest who have died in the faith — a great partnership, a communion, and an indestructible family — God's own people — the saints. Psalm 116 puts it: "Precious in the sight of the Lord is the death of his saints" (RSV).

In the preface before communion we say, "Therefore with angels and archangels and with all the company of Heaven, we laud and magnify his glorious name, evermore praising thee...."

One saint's death — Roberta Keller — baptized April 5, 1913, by the Rev. Simon Peter Long here where she died, has reminded us in a dramatic way:

5. We are the communion of saints.
4. We believe in the resurrection of the body and the life everlasting.
3. Life is uncertain and our task urgent.
2. We have a gift to give.
1. Our worship has grave implications.

Paul sums it up for us: "So, my dear brothers, since future victory is sure, be strong and steady, always abounding in the Lord's work, for you know nothing you do for the Lord is ever wasted as it would be if there were no resurrection" (1 Corinthians 15:58, TLB). The last hymn we sang last Sunday was "Come Down, O Love Divine." After praying for the comfort of Mrs. Keller's family, we closed our service by singing:

Come down, O Love divine, Seek thou this soul of mine
And visit it with thine own ardor glowing;
O Comforter, draw near, within my heart appear
And kindle it, thy holy flame bestowing.

(Reprinted from "Through The Valley Of The Shadow," CSS Publishing Company, Inc., © 1976.)

20

God Promises, Promises!

John R. Brokhoff

John 14:2-3 (KJV)

> *In my Father's house are many mansions; if it were not so, I would have told you. I go to prepare a place for you. And if I go and prepare a place for you, I will come again, and receive you unto myself; that where I am, there ye may be also.*

A former student of mine tells this boyhood experience about his father's promises. When he was an eight-year-old lad, his father promised him a BB gun for which he longed with intense desire. His dad promised that when his next paycheck came, they would get the gun. In those days, work was scarce and his father only had a part-time state job. On the day when the check was due to arrive, it rained and the road was muddy. The check came on time, but with it was a letter ordering him to come to Atlanta, 200 miles away, that very day. The boy knew that his father could not drive in the rain to town twenty miles away, come back with a gun, and then drive to Atlanta. To keep his father from seeing his disappointment, he slipped up to his room and sobbed with a broken heart. He heard his mother and dad whispering to each other while his mother packed a bag for his father. Then he heard the front door slam and the leaving of the car. He wept himself almost to sleep, but sometime later he was awakened by a familiar sound of a horn. It was his dad. He rushed to the front porch and saw his dad holding out a BB gun to him. He ran down and took it. Neither he nor his father had a word to say. There was no need of saying anything. His dad drove off to Atlanta. Years later, the student, now a prominent minister, said that when anyone said anything about the promises of the Heavenly Father, he had no difficulty believing them because he had this experience with his earthly father's promises. If an earthly father could keep his promises, how much more would the Heavenly Father keep his promises!

On this occasion, when our hearts are broken because of the loss of a loved one, we hear some promises of the Father through his Son, Jesus Christ. These promises, if accepted and trusted, will bring us comfort and peace in our sadness.

In our text Jesus promises us that there is room in heaven for all of God's people. He said, "In my Father's house there are many mansions...." In other words, there is room for everyone who dies in Christ. It is not true that heaven has a limited enrollment. We cannot say that only 144,000 are allowed to be in heaven. Heaven is big enough for all those who put their trust in God.

Isn't this good news for us who sorrow over the passing of a loved one? We need not worry whether there was room for him. All of us know that when we take a trip to an important and popular place (Heaven is as popular a place as one can find, for who does not want to go to Heaven?) that there is always a question whether or not we will be able to get reservations. Usually we seek reservations weeks in advance to be sure there will be a place or room for us. The marvelous thing about this promise is that we need not make reservations with God to get living space in heaven. There is room for all who die in Christ. No one will be left out. God will not treat any of his children like men once treated his Son when there was no room in the inn for Jesus to be born.

In our text, Jesus makes another promise to us. He tells us that he is going ahead of us to prepare a place for us in heaven. Hear his words: "I go to prepare a place for you."

In human relations we know that when we expect visitors or guests in our homes, we make preparations for them. We stock up on food and drink so that there will be plenty on hand when the guests arrive. The house is given a good cleaning. Special meals are prepared. Before guests arrive, the house is in a hubbub of preparation. If this is the case with human guests in our homes, would it also not be true that God through Jesus makes preparations for his children to come to their eternal home? What kind of preparation does Jesus make for us to come to heaven? It is a spiritual preparation.

The preparation is necessary because the Bible tells us that when every one of us dies, we must appear before God, the righteous judge. God is infinite and holy. We are finite and sinful. We cannot stand before Almighty God in our own right, dressed in the filthy rags of our unworthiness and sins. Jesus has gone ahead to make things right with God. He made these preparations when he was on earth by dying on the cross for our sins and rising from the dead that we too might rise from death. On earth he fulfilled all the laws of God and completed all of God's demands of perfection. Now Jesus goes to God in heaven and says that in behalf of all men he has died for their sins and completed for man all that God asked of man. He begs God to forgive men on the basis of his own work and merits. That is why we say Jesus is our Mediator. He intercedes for us before God and he makes it possible for us to stand before God with the robe of righteousness given to us by Christ. When we die and appear before God, everything has been taken care of that we might be admitted to God's presence and accepted in love for Jesus' sake.

Is this truly not a comfort to each of us sinners? Now we need not worry about our loved ones or ourselves whom we confess to be sinners. For who is perfect? Jesus promised that he would go ahead and prepare a place for us in God's kingdom. To trust this promise will bring us comfort and encouragement.

In the words of Jesus, our text tells us of a third promise of the Father through Jesus. It is the promise that Jesus will be with us. That we will not be alone in heaven. Listen to the promise, "Where I am, there ye may be also."

We do not know who is going to be in heaven, except One. This one is Jesus himself. Indeed, there will be others, but no one can be certain that our friends and members of the family will be there. That is in God's hands. We can be sure that Jesus is there and that really is enough.

Have you ever wondered what heaven is like? Is it a place of pearly gates and streets of gold? Does anyone know about the "furniture" of heaven? No one can say what heaven is like. All we can do is paint pictures involving symbolism. But one thing we can be sure of: Christ promises that he will be there to greet and meet us when we arrive and ever stay with us. That is what makes Heaven. It is not necessarily a physical place with all kinds of jewels. It is a spiritual condition made possible by the presence of Jesus. Where he is, there is life and love and peace. Then to be in Heaven means to be in life, to be in love, to be at peace in Christ. Since this is so, why then should we lament the passing of a loved one who died in Christ? This dear one is far better off than we are on earth. He is experiencing the time of his life. He is saying, "This is real living!" Heaven is a glorious place where love, life, and joy abound.

You know, a promise is only as good as the one who makes it. Who made these promises about our going to heaven? It is none other than God speaking through Jesus to his disciples. Is there anyone greater or more trustworthy than God? Even if a great and reliable person makes a promise, we believe a promise until the time the person making the promise does not keep it. After that, we doubt whether any future promise will be kept. Can anyone ever claim that God at any one time or place ever broke a promise to man? Indeed, the truth is that God has always kept his Word. He will keep it now, and will always keep his Word. God is not capricious. God is steadfast, constant, and forever dependable. You can trust these promises of Christ. If you stand on these promises, you will have comfort and strength, not only now in this hour of bereavement, but in all the days ahead.

(Reprinted from "Through The Valley Of The Shadow," CSS Publishing Company, Inc., © 1976.)